Alessandra Avallone

pizza
& focaccia

Photography **Francesca Moscheni**

BIBLIOTHECA CULINARIA

Pizza or focaccia?

The difference between the two is not entirely clear, even for Italians. Each regional cuisine has its own interpretations in addition to the inevitable linguistic borrowings and overlapping. For example, what is known as "pizza" in Bari, turns out to be "focaccia with tomatoes" in Milan. In simple (but not absolute) terms, one could say that a focaccia has no tomato-sauce. Without a doubt the first pizza was similarly sauceless, if you like, the result of its evolutionary "Big Bang" was a focaccia, probably topped only with extra virgin olive oil and salt. Bakers created this product to test the temperature of their wood-fired ovens before beginning to bake bread. The more elaborate toppings came later, evolving according to the seasonal availibility of produce, the bakers' imagination or their customers' tastes.

Making pizza at home means you may choose the best ingredients and apply your own personal touch. From the dough to the final topping, give your imagination free rein and you won't find yourself alone in the kitchen. Bear in mind, however, that you shouldn't overdo it: two or three "important" flavours are more than enough to create a balanced taste. Given that pizza loves company, both children and guests will be happy to try their luck at putting together a signature pizza. You will also discover that the–aroma–of pizza cooking in the oven (or on a barbeque) has a wonderful power to bring friends together.

Preparing basic pizza dough

The pizzas and focaccias presented in this book may be prepared with any of the following basic dough recipes. Your choice will depend on the amount of time at your disposal and on personal taste. The quantities given will make two or three thin crusted pizzas, one thick focaccia or filled pizza or eight pizza strips or mini pizzas.

Using a pizza stone will guarantee even cooking and consistent results (see page 7). There are two ways to organize preparation: you can preheat the pizza stone, as indicated in the recipes, or assemble your pizza directly on the cold pizza stone, in which case, you will need to add 5-10 minutes to the overall cooking time. Do remember to preheat the oven and position the rack in the lower portion.The temperature should always be quite high: 220 °C (430 °F) for the thickest focaccias (30-40 minutes baking time) and 240-250 °C (460-480 °F) for thin and crisp pizzas which cook quickly (10 minutes baking time) You will find precise cooking times within each individual recipe that follows.

Quick basic pizza dough

Yields approximately 800 g
(1 ³/₄ lbs) of dough:

500 g (1 ¹/₄ lb) plain flour
+ flour for your work surface
8 g (¹/₄ oz) dried brewer's yeast
or 20 g (³/₄ oz) fresh brewer's yeast
250 ml (1 cup) warm water
1 tsp coarse sea salt
1 tbsp extra virgin olive oil

1 Make a mound with 500 g (1 ¼ lb) of flour in a bowl or on your work surface. Create a small well in the centre and add the yeast (8 g / ¹/₄ oz dry or 20 g / ³/₄ oz fresh). Pour in 100 ml (a little less than ¹/₂ cup) lukewarm water to dissolve the yeast. Cover the mixture and let it stand for 5 minutes.

2 Sprinkle 1 teaspoon of coarse sea salt over the flour.* Add 1 tbsp of extra virgin olive oil and the remaining water. Knead the dough until it forms a smooth and firm ball, coat it with a little oil and cover with a damp cloth or with an overturned bowl.

*Avoid direct contact between the yeast, a "living" organism and the salt, as the latter will damage it and prevent the dough from rising properly.

3 Allow the dough to rise for 30 minutes at room temperature. If you want to make mini focaccias or mini pizzas, divide the dough into the required number of portions and let them rise until they double in volume.

4 If you prefer to make a large pizza or focaccia to cook on the pizza stone, let the dough rise completely, for about 1 hour and 15 minutes (in addition to the 30 minutes required in step 3).

5 Flatten out the dough on a floured work surface stretching it several times with your hands or a rolling pin. Pause for a few minutes between the start and finish of each operation so that the dough can lose some of its elasticity.

6 Transfer the pizza or focaccia to the hot, previously greased or floured pizza stone. Add your preferred topping and bake immediately. Alternatively, you can roll out the dough on a sheet of baking parchment and use it to transfer the pizza or the focaccia to the the hot stone. This method is particularly useful when the weight of the topping is considerable.

Slow-rising basic pizza dough [Yields approximately 900 g (2 lb) of dough]

500 g (1 ¼ lb) plain flour + flour for kneading
4 g (⅛ oz) dried brewer's yeast
350 ml (1 ½ cups) warm water

1 tsp coarse sea salt
1 tbsp extra virgin olive oil

Measure the flour into a bowl. Make a small well in the centre and pour in the lukewarm water. Dissolve the yeast in the water, cover the bowl with a cloth and let it rest for 15 minutes.

Sprinkle the salt over the flour (see note on page 4). Combine the flour with the water and yeast mixture until you obtain dough that is somewhat sticky and uneven. Cover again with the cloth and let the dough rest again for 30 minutes.

Dust the work surface with abundant flour. Tip the dough onto it, dust it with flour and fold it in three by bringing the edges in towards the middle. Turn the dough 90°, dust it again with flour and fold it in three. Repeat this operation until the dough no longer sticks (another 3-4 times) but don't knead it.

Place the dough in an oiled bowl. Turn it over to coat it evenly and cover it with a sheet of baking parchment that has been dampened and wrung out, and then with a damp cloth. Place the bowl in the least cold compartment of the refrigerator and let it rest for 12 hours.

Remove the dough from the refrigerator. Flatten it with the palm of your hand before reshaping it into a ball and allowing it to rest in a warm place for 1 hour before using it. If you want to make a round thin-crusted pizza, divide the dough into 3 portions. Stretch each portion out one at a time on your work surface, spreading them with your hands covered in flour. Add the topping and follow the baking instructions presented in your chosen recipe.

Wholemeal pizza dough [Yields approximately 900 g (2 lb) of dough]

500 g (1 ¼ lb) wholemeal flour + flour for kneading
350 ml (1 ½ cups) warm water
8 g (¼ oz) dried brewer's yeast or 20 g (¾ oz) fresh brewer's yeast

1 tsp coarse sea salt
1 tsp honey
2-3 tbsp extra virgin olive oil

Mix the flour and salt in a bowl. Make a small well in the centre. Dissolve the yeast and honey in the warm water. Cover it and let it rest for 10 minutes. Pour the liquid into the well in the flour, mixing it in a little at a time with a wooden spoon. Transfer the dough to a floured work surface and knead it until it is smooth and even, incorporating 2-3 tablespoons of extra virgin olive oil in the process. Shape the dough into a ball. Cover it and allow it to rise for 30 minutes. Knead it again briefly and let it rise again until it doubles in volume.

Divide the dough into the number of pizzas or focaccias you want to make. Let it rise again for 10 minutes before rolling out the pizzas and continuing with the desired toppings. Follow the baking instructions presented in your chosen recipe.

Cooked to perfection

A pizza that has been cooked properly has a crisp crust, but not a dry topping. With respect to a pizzeria, baking in a domestic oven often leaves much to be desired. The time/temperature ratio is tricky and the results can be very inconsistent.

The Emile Henry® pizza stone is the perfect tool for obtaining professional results from your home oven. Manufactured in ceramic with the proprietary Flame® glaze, it ensures a more even distribution of heat than may be achieved with traditional metal trays. As a result, the base of the pizza cooks quickly and evenly without sacrificing the more delicate ingredients of the topping. Lighter than traditional earthenware oven stones and designed with ergonomic grips, it is also much easier to handle. The absence of a raised edge makes it easier to cut a pizza directly on the stone while the glaze, perfected by the manufacturer, not only makes it highly heat resistant, but also protects it from scratches and chipping. This versatile cooking tool is suitable for use under the grill, on the barbeque and in the microwave. It is also dishwasher safe.

Available in four colours and two sizes (Ø 35.5 cm / 14 in and Ø 25.5 cm / 10 in), the pizza stone lends itself to additional uses. Given its resistence to cutting instruments, it can double as a cheese platter. It's great for presenting hors d'oeuvres and, naturally, for serving the perfect pizza: you'll discover the heat retained by the stone keeps pizza hot and steaming.

Pizza Margherita plus

For **4** servings
Preparation:
5 minutes
Cooking time:
15 minutes

300 g (10,5 oz) basic pizza
dough (see recipes on pages
4-6)
250 g (9 oz) tomato purée
150 g (5 ¹/₂ oz) well-drained
cow's milk mozzarella
4 *bocconcini* of buffalo milk
mozzarella*
a few sprigs of basil
4-8 slices of prosciutto crudo
(or other dry-cured ham)
extra virgin olive oil
salt
freshly ground pepper

*Italian for bite-sized,
bocconcini are miniature
mozzarelle, often sold as
"cocktail mozzarella."

Preheat the oven to 250 °C (480 °F).

Dice the cow's milk mozzarella and salt the tomato puree.
Using your hands or a rolling pin, stretch the pizza dough on a floured
work surface giving it a circular form identical to that of the pizza stone.

Transfer the dough to the preheated pizza stone and top it with a thin
layer of tomato purée. Drizzle with extra virgin olive oil and transfer to
the hot oven for 5 minutes. Remove the pizza, evenly distribute the diced
mozzarella over the surface and return it to the oven. Continue cooking
for approximately 10 minutes.

Immediately upon removing the pizza from the oven, distribute the basil
leaves over the surface and divide the pizza into 4 portions. Garnish each
with a *bocconcino* of mozzarella and one or two slices of prosciutto. Season with freshly ground pepper and serve immediately.

Pissaladière

Preheat the oven to 200 °C (390 °F).

For 8 servings
Preparation:
15 minutes
Cooking time:
40 minutes
(onions)
40 minutes
(pissaladière)

250 g (9 oz) basic pizza dough
(see recipes on pages 4-6)
1 kg (2 $^1/_4$ lbs) yellow onions
14 oil-packed anchovy fillets
40 g (1 $^1/_2$ oz) black olives
(preferably of the taggiasche
or niçoise variety)
extra virgin olive oil
coarse sea salt

Peel the onions, cut them in half and slice them thinly. Transfer to a large frying pan with a ladleful of water and a few tablespoons of extra virgin olive oil. Cook over low heat for 30 minutes, adding more water should the onions begin to dry out.

Move the onions to one side of the pan and add two more tablespoons of oil and 4 anchovy fillets. Use a wooden spoon to crush them and combine them with the oil. Once they have completely disintegrated, blend with the onions and continue cooking for 10 minutes over low heat. The onions should achieve a meltingly smooth texture without becoming dry. Season with salt and pepper.

Using your hands or a rolling pin, stretch the pizza dough on a floured work surface giving it a circular form while keeping it thicker at the edges. Dust the preheated pizza stone with flour. Transfer the dough to the stone and top it with the onion mixture to within 1 $^1/_4$ cm ($^1/_2$ inch) from the edge. Arrange the remaining anchovy fillets radiating from the centre.

Bake the pissaladière for 30 minutes. Add the olives, distributing them evenly and continue cooking for another 10 minutes. Serve warm or cold.

Wholemeal focaccia with cherry tomatoes

For **8** servings
Preparation:
15 minutes
Resting time:
15 minutes
Cooking time:
approx. 45 minutes

450 g (1 lb)
wholemeal pizza dough
(see page 6)
300 g (10 ½ oz) cherry
tomatoes
a few sprigs of fresh rosemary
2 cloves of garlic
extra virgin olive oil
coarse sea salt

Preheat the oven to 220 °C (430 °F).

Using your hands or a rolling pin, stretch the pizza dough on a floured work surface forming a disc with a diameter of 30 cm (12 in).

Wash and dry the cherry tomatoes. Cut them in half and embed them in the dough with the cut side facing upwards. Peel the garlic and slice it finely. Embed a slice next to each tomato half. Drizzle generously with extra virgin olive oil and sprinkle with rosemary needles and freshly ground coarse salt. Allow to rest for 15 minutes.

Transfer the focaccia to the preheated stone and bake for approximately 45 minutes.

Pizza with curly endive

For 4-6 servings
Preparation:
40 minutes
Cooking time:
10 minutes
(vegetables)
35 minutes
(pizza)

400 g (14 oz) basic or
wholemeal pizza dough
(see recipes on pages 4-6)
2 heads of curly endive (frisée)
1 white onion
2 cloves of garlic
100 g black olives
(Gaeta or Kalamata)
2 tbsp capers in vinegar
80 g semi mature Pecorino
extra virgin olive oil
salt
freshly ground pepper

Preheat the oven to 220 °C (430 °F).

With your hands or a rolling pin stretch the pizza dough to form a disc that is at least 2,5-3 cm (1-1 ½ in) larger than the pizza stone.

Wash the endive and break it up with your hands. Heat 2 tablespoons of extra virgin olive oil in a large frying pan. Add the unpeeled garlic cloves and sauté them briefly. Add the endive and salt and cook over high heat until the greens wilt. Use a spoon to remove about ½ cup (120 ml) of the cooking liquid from the pan and reserve it; allow the remainder to evaporate. Add the olives and capers to the endive. Remove the garlic and transfer the contents of the frying pan to a plate to cool.

Slice the onion and sauté it in the same pan in one tablespoon of extra virgin olive oil until it just begins to colour. Salt lightly.

Coarsely grate half the cheese over the dough. Top with the cooked endive arranging it largely in the centre. Add the cooked onions and the remaining cheese, distributing them evenly. Fold the uncovered edges of the dough inward to partially cover the filling.

Transfer the pizza to the preheated stone. Emulsify the reserved cooking liquid from the endive with 1 tablespoon of extra virgin olive oil and brush the dough with this mixture. Bake the pizza at 220 °C (430 °F) for 30-35 minutes.

Pizza strips
with courgette/zucchini ribbons and burrata

For 4 servings
Preparation:
20 minutes
Rising time:
(additional) 20 minutes
Cooking time:
20 minutes

350 g (12 oz) basic pizza
dough (see recipes
on pages 4-6)
2 courgettes/zucchini
2 thin spring onions
10-12 dried tomatoes in oil
1/2 lemon
300 g (10 1/2 oz) burrata*
extra virgin olive oil
salt

*A specialty of the Puglia
region, burrata is similar to
mozzarella. Produced from
cow's milk or buffalo milk, its
shiny, elastic interior conceals
a cream-filled centre. You
can produce a similar, buttery
texture by breaking up fresh
mozzarella and allowing it to
"marinate" in fresh cream for
a few hours.

Preheat the oven to 220 °C (430 °F).

Divide the pizza dough into 8 equal portions. Cover them with a cloth and allow them to rise for 20 minutes. With your hands or a rolling pin stretch out each portion of dough into a long, narrow tongue-shaped strip. Transfer these to the preheated pizza stone, drizzle with extra virgin olive oil and sprinkle with a little water. Bake in a preheated oven for 15 minutes.

Meanwhile, break up the dried tomatoes. Wash the courgettes/zucchini and, without peeling them, slice them into ribbons. Slice the spring onions diagonally. Season the courgette/zucchini and spring onions with salt, a little extra virgin olive oil and a splash of lemon juice.

Evenly distribute the vegetables over the pizza strips and return them to the oven for 5 minutes. While they are still very hot, top them with spoonfuls of the burrata and serve immediately.

You may replace the burrata with cubes of olive tofu for a tasty vegan alternative.

Pizza with courgette/zucchini flowers

For **2** servings
Preparation:
10 minutes
Cooking time:
20 minutes

200 g (7 oz) basic pizza dough
(see recipes on pages 4-6)
4 tbsp tomato purée
12 grape tomatoes
1 courgette/zucchini
6 courgette/zucchini flowers
160 g (5 ½ oz) well-drained
diced mozzarella or provola*
30 g Parmigiano
2 sprigs of fresh mint
extra virgin olive oil
salt
freshly ground pepper

*A "pulled" or "stretched"
cheese made from buffalo or
cow's milk, often available in
a smoked version.

Preheat the oven to 220 °C (430 °F) with two individual pizza stones.

Divide the dough in two equal portions and with your hands or a rolling pin stretch them to form two discs roughly the same size as the pizza stones.

Gently wash the zucchini flowers, pat them dry with paper towels and remove the pistils. Stuff the flowers with the diced mozzarella.

Thinly slice the courgettes/zucchini with a mandoline or a vegetable peeler. Halve the grape tomatoes. Transfer the discs of pizza dough to the preheated stones. Top with a thin layer of tomato purée, the grape tomatoes and the courgette/zucchini ribbons.

Season with salt, a drizzle of extra virgin olive oil and bake in a preheated oven for 10 minutes. Remove the pizzas and arrange three stuffed courgette/zucchini flowers on each. Return them to the oven for an additional 10 minutes to complete cooking.

Fresh from the oven, garnish with shavings of Parmigiano, the mint leaves and a drizzle of extra virgin olive oil. Finish with freshly ground pepper, if you wish.

You may produce a non-vegetarian version of this pizza by introducing a single oil-preserved anchovy into each courgette/zucchini flower together with the mozzarella cubes.

"Black" focaccia with panzanella

For **6-8** servings
Preparation:
15 minutes
Rising time:
45 minutes
Cooking time:
30 minutes

450 g (1 lb) slow-rising pizza dough (see recipe on page 6) kneaded with 3 tbsp highest quality black olive paste
200 g (7 oz) tomato purée

For the panzanella*:
300 g (10 ½ oz) fresh tuna fillets
1 small cucumber
2 semi-ripe tomatoes
2 tender celery stalks
1 small purple onion
2-3 tbsp black olives
1 chilli pepper
1 clove of garlic
2 sprigs of basil
red wine vinegar
extra virgin olive oil
salt

*A Tuscan specialty typically made of torn, dried bread topped with a salad of fresh tomatoes, onions, etc. liberally seasoned with extra virgin olive oil and red wine vinegar.

Preheat the oven to 220 °C (430 °F).

Using your hands or a rolling pin stretch the dough on a floured sheet of baking parchment forming a disc roughly the same size as the pizza stone. Pat it down gently and allow it to rise again for about 30 minutes under a clean cloth. Dip your fingers in oil and make small dimples all over the dough. Spread with a thin layer of the salted tomato purée and leave it to rise again for another 15 minutes.

Transfer the focaccia to the preheated, lightly greased pizza stone and bake in a hot oven for 30-40 minutes.

Finely slice the garlic and the chilli pepper and leave them to marinate in a small bowl of extra virgin olive oil along with a few chopped basil leaves.

In the meantime, cook the tuna fish in a dry frying pan for 30 seconds on each side. Allow it to cool before cutting it into small cubes and seasoning it with salt and a drizzle of extra virgin olive oil.

Wash the vegetables. Cut the tomatoes into wedges; dice the celery and cucumber. Mix them with the black olives and the onion slices separated into rings. Season the salad with the flavoured oil, salt and vinegar to taste. Combine with the tuna fish.

Slice the warm focaccia. Top it with the tuna salad and a few basil leaves and serve.

The tuna may be replaced with, mackerel or fine quality sardines preserved in oil or even fresh, raw anchovies marinated in lemon juice.
Omit the fish for a vegan version of this recipe, adding instead 2 tablespoons of capers to the salad.

Ligurian-style focaccia with cheese

For **4-6** servings
Preparation:
10 minutes
Cooking time:
approx. 15 minutes

350 g (12 oz) basic pizza
dough (see recipes
on pages 4-6)
300 g (10 ½ oz) Crescenza*
(or ricotta or quark)
extra virgin olive oil
salt
freshly ground pepper

*A fresh cow's milk cheese
with a relatively high water/
low fat ratio. Rapidly maturing
(7-8 days), it has a creamy
texture and a sweet flavour.

Preheat the oven to 220 °C (430 °F).

Divide the dough into 2 equal portions. Roll out the first into a very thin disc on a well-floured work surface.

Transfer the dough to the preheated pizza stone dusted with flour. Quickly spread the crumbled cheese over the dough. Roll out the second portion of dough in the same way and place it over the cheese.

Roll the edges of the dough towards the centre to seal them. With a sharp knife make a few slits in the top layer to allow steam to escape and immediately transfer the focaccia to the preheated oven. Bake for approximately 15 minutes or until golden and the cheese is completely melted.

Finish with a dusting of freshly ground pepper and serve immediately.

Alternatively, you may prepare the focaccia on a sheet of floured baking parchment and slide it onto the preheated pizza stone just before baking.

Panzerotti with ricotta and greens

For **6** servings
Preparation:
30 minutes
Cooking time:
10 minutes
(greens)
15 minutes
(panzerotti)

300 g (12 oz) basic pizza
dough (see recipes
on pages 4-6)
250 g (9 oz) sheep's milk
ricotta
250 g (9 oz) swiss chard leaves
(or spinach or broccoli rabe)
60 g (2 oz) grated semi-mature
Pecorino
1 dried red chilli pepper
1/2 clove of garlic
1 tbsp tomato purée
extra virgin olive oil
coarse sea salt

Preheat the oven to 220 °C (430 °F).

Wash the greens and trim them eliminating any tough stems; cut them into small pieces. In a frying pan heat 2 tablespoons of extra virgin olive oil and add the chopped garlic and half of the chilli pepper. Follow with the greens and season with salt. Cover and continue cooking for a few minutes or just long enough to wilt the greens. Uncover the pan and allow the water released by the leaves to evaporate.

Thinly roll out the pizza dough on a floured work surface. Use a pastry cutter to cut out a dozen discs with a diameter of 10-12 cm (4-5 in). Place a small amount of the cooked greens, a tablespoon of ricotta and a pinch of grated Pecorino in the centre of each disc. Fold them in half and pinch along the edges to seal them perfectly.

Mix the tomato purée with a tablespoon of extra virgin olive oil. Dust the preheated pizza stone with flour. Arrange the panzerotti on it and brush them quickly with the tomato-oil emulsion. Bake them for 15 minutes and serve hot or warm.

Rolled pizza with sausage

For **6-8** servings
Preparation:
25 minutes
Resting time:
15 minutes
Cooking time:
20 minutes (sausage)
45 minutes (pizza)

450 g (1 lb) slow-rising pizza
dough (see recipe on page 6)
flour for the work surface
200 g (7 oz) sausages
400 g (14 oz) broccoli rabe
(or broccoli)
1 organic lemon
1 organic orange
1 tsp toasted fennel seeds
150 g (5 ½ oz) well-drained
mozzarella or provola*
extra virgin olive oil
salt
freshly ground pepper

*See note on page 18.

Preheat the oven to 220 °C (430 °F).

Roll out the pizza dough on a floured work surface creating a rectangular shape. Cut a thin strip from the long side of the dough and reserve. Transfer the dough to a sheet of baking parchment dusted with flour.

Blanch the broccoli rabe (or broccoli) in boiling salted water. Drain and squeeze out as much excess water as possible before chopping coarsely.

Remove the casings from the sausages and crumble the meat. Grate the rind of half a lemon and half an orange over the sausage, add freshly ground pepper to taste and a teaspoon of toasted fennel seeds. Brown the sausage in a frying pan without oil. When it begins to colour, remove it with a slotted spoon in order to eliminate as much excess fat as possible.

Distribute the sausage over the dough. Top with the broccoli rabe (or broccoli) and the sliced cheese. Roll the dough, beginning from the longest side, and tuck in the ends to seal them. Bind it with the reserved strip of dough and position the roll with the seam-side down.

Emulsify 2 tablespoons of extra virgin olive oil with 1 tablespoon of lemon juice, 2 tablespoons of orange juice and a pinch of salt. Brush the pizza with this mixture and transfer it with the baking parchment to the preheated pizza stone. Bake at 220 °C (430 °F) for 45 minutes.

Allow the pizza to rest for 15 minutes before slicing. Serve topped with the remaining freshly grated citrus rind.

Tomato and double aubergine/ eggplant pizza

For **6** servings
Preparation:
25 minutes + 12 hours
to drain the yoghurt
Cooking time:
20 minutes
(aubergine/eggplant)
20 minutes
(pizza)

400 g (14 oz) basic pizza
dough (see recipes
on pages 4-6)
150 g (5 ½ oz) tomato purée
1 long aubergine/eggplant
1 round aubergine/eggplant
1 clove of garlic
600 g (22 oz) full fat
natural yoghurt
1 bunch of fresh basil
1 pinch of hot red chili flakes
extra virgin olive oil
salt

Mix the yoghurt with 2 pinches of salt and place in a strainer lined with cheesecloth. Leave to drain for 12 hours in the refrigerator until it becomes thick and creamy.

Preheat the oven to 180 °C (350 °F).
Coat the round aubergine/eggplant with a little oil and bake for 20 minutes or until it becomes tender. Leave it to cool then peel it and mash the pulp with a fork. Season it with the garlic crushed with a pinch of coarse salt, a pinch of hot red chili flakes, a few basil leaves and a tablespoon of extra virgin olive oil. Raise the oven temperature to 220 °C (430 °F).

Wash the long aubergine/eggplant and thinly slice it without peeling. Fry the slices in extra virgin olive oil until crisp and drain the "chips" on paper towels. Salt lightly and reserve.

With your hands or a rolling pin, flatten the dough on a floured work surface working from the centre outward so that the perimeter of the disc remains somewhat thicker. Transfer it to the preheated pizza stone. Spread the tomato purée over the dough. Season with salt and bake in the hot oven at 220 °C (430 °F) for 20 minutes or until the crust is well cooked and golden.

Top the freshly baked pizza with spoonfuls of the mashed aubergine/eggplant, the yoghurt cheese, the aubergine/eggplant "chips" and fresh basil leaves. Serve immediately.

Pizza with marinated fresh anchovies

For **6** servings
Preparation:
35 minutes
Marinating time:
10 minutes
Cooking time:
15 minutes

300 g (10 ½ oz) white or wholemeal pizza dough (see recipes on pages 4-6)
flour for your work surface
24 fresh anchovies
or small sardines
1 purple onion
1 organic lemon
1 tsp fennel seeds
1 tsp dried oregano
extra virgin olive oil
fine salt

Preheat the oven to 220 °C (430 °F).

Remove the heads, eviscerate and debone the fish. Rinse them thoroughly. Place them in a single layer in a glass or ceramic dish and sprinkle them with 2-3 tablespoons of fine salt. Refrigerate for 10 minutes. Rinse the fish well to remove the salt and pat them dry with paper towels. Season with 3 tablespoons of extra virgin olive oil.

Finely slice the onion and the lemon.

Roll out the dough on a floured work surface to form a thin, rectangular sheet. Let it rest for 10 minutes covered with a cloth. Divide the dough into smaller rectangles 12-15 cm (5-6 in) on the long side and arrange them on the preheated pizza stone. Bake in the preheated oven for 10 minutes.

Take the stone out of the oven. Place 2 anchovies (or sardines) on each portion of dough, add 1 slice of lemon, a few onion rings, a pinch of fennel seeds and dried oregano. Drizzle with extra virgin olive oil and return to a very hot oven or place under the broiler (grill) for 3-4 minutes.
Serve immediately.

Mini potato focaccias

Preheat the oven to 220 °C (430 °F).

Cook the potatoes in boiling salted water until they are tender. Drain, peel and mash them then allow them to cool.

For **6-8** servings
Preparation:
20 minutes + 2 hours
of rising time
Cooking time:
30 minutes
(potatoes)
15 minutes
(mini focacce)

600 g (1 $\frac{1}{3}$ lbs) all-purpose
flour
200 g (7 oz) potatoes
25 g (1 oz) fresh brewer's yeast
extra virgin olive oil
fine salt
sea salt

Dissolve the yeast in $\frac{1}{4}$ cup (60 ml) of warm water. Sift the flour on your work surface and create a well in the centre. Transfer the mashed potato and yeast into this depression in the flour. Sprinkle 1 teaspoon of salt over perimeter of the flour*. Knead the mixture just enough to combine the ingredients adding more warm water as necessary to obtain a soft dough. Knead for about 10 minutes. Transfer the dough to a bowl. Cover it with a cloth and let it rise until it doubles in volume.

Divide the dough into 12-16 small balls. Dust them with flour and let them rest for 10 minutes before rolling them out. Cut 3 or 4 slits in each with the tip of a sharp knife. Coat your fingers with flour and use them to enlarge the openings.

Arrange the mini-focaccias on 2 preheated pizza stones. Working quickly, brush them with an emulsion of equal parts of extra virgin olive oil and water and sprinkle with a few grains of sea salt. Let them rest for 10 minutes before baking for approximately 15 minutes.

Serve the mini focaccias with goat cheese, olives and a glass of *pastis or anisette*.

Avoid direct contact between the salt and the yeast, a "living" organism, as it will be damaged and prevent the dough from rising properly.

Pizza strips with radicchio, Brie, mushrooms and crispy speck

For 4 servings
Preparation:
10 minutes
Resting time:
15 minutes
Cooking time:
3 minutes (radicchio)
20 minutes (pizza)

250 g (9 oz) basic pizza dough
(see recipes on pages 4-6)
1 head of Treviso radicchio
(or chicory or frisée)
200 g (7 oz) Brie
(or similar semi-soft white
rinded cheese)
4 slices of speck (or pancetta
or smoked bacon)
1 fresh porcini mushroom
(or a few slices of frozen
porcini mushrooms, or 4 very
fresh white mushrooms)
30 g (1 oz) of Parmigiano
150 ml (²/₃ cup) white
wine vinegar
extra virgin olive oil
salt
freshly ground pepper

Preheat the oven to 220 °C (430 °F).

Separate the radicchio leaves. Bring a small saucepan of salted water to a boil then add the vinegar. Submerge the radicchio leaves for 3 minutes; drain and transfer to a plate. Drizzle the leaves with extra virgin olive oil and set them aside until they cool completely (you may prepare the radicchio 1 or 2 days in advance and keep it in the refrigerator).

Allow the ball of dough to rest for 15 minutes. Cut it in half. Dust your hands in flour and stretch each piece of dough gently to obtain 2 long and thin tongue-shaped strips.

Transfer the dough strips to the preheated pizza stone. Top each with 3 small slices of Brie, a few radicchio leaves and a slice of speck cut into 3 or 4 pieces.

Bake in a preheated oven for 15 minutes. Remove the pizza strips from the oven and add the (fresh or frozen) slices of porcini mushrooms or the sliced white mushrooms and season with salt and pepper. Return to the oven for an additional 5 minutes.

Just out of the oven, top the pizza strips with small flakes of Parmigiano and a generous amount of freshly ground pepper. Serve immediately.

Omit the speck to make a vegetarian version or omit the speck and cheese while doubling the quantity of radicchio and mushrooms to make a vegan version.

Pizza with leeks, squash hummus and salami

Preheat the oven to 220 °C (430 °F).

For **8** servings
Preparation:
25 minutes
Rising time:
(additional) 15 minutes
Cooking time:
40 minutes

450 g (1 lb) basic or
wholemeal pizza dough
(see recipes on pages 4-6)
1 large leek
80 g (3 oz) artisanal salami
(or raw-cured or smoked ham
or prosciutto).
300 g (10 ½ oz) flesh of
butternut or delicata squash
1 clove of garlic
1 sprig of rosemary
1 tablespoon of tahini
(sesame paste)
1 bunch of fresh young sage
extra virgin olive oil
salt
hot red chili flakes

Using your hands or a rolling pin flatten the dough on a sheet of floured baking parchment to make a pizza ½ cm (¼ in) thick. Cover it and let it rise for 15 minutes. Dimple the surface with your fingertips.

Finely slice the white portion of the leek and season it with an emulsion of extra virgin olive oil and 1-2 tablespoons of salted water. Spread the leeks over the surface of the dough and bake at 220 °C (430 °F) for 40 minutes or until the pizza has turned golden and has risen well.

In the meantime, cut the squash flesh into cubes and transfer it a roasting tin along with the sliced garlic, a drizzle of olive oil, salt and rosemary. Bake on the top oven rack for 20 minutes (the pizza will already be cooking on the lower rack). When the squash is tender, transfer it to a blender or robot and process with the tahini. Add a pinch of hot red chili and salt to taste.

Blanch the sage leaves for 1 minute in boiling salted water. Drain them and chop them coarsely. Place them in the blender or robot together with 5 tablespoons of extra virgin olive oil and emulsify.

When the pizza is cooked, top it with thin slices of salami and the sage infused oil. Accompany it with the squash hummus.

If you prefer to serve the pizza as a snack, cut it into squares and heap a teaspoonful of hummus on each piece.
For a vegan version, add only a drop of oil to the sage and omit the salami slices.

Mini focaccias with spring onions, mozzarella and cherry tomato confit

For **8** servings
Preparation:
20 minutes
Rising time:
15 minutes
Cooking time:
1 hour
(cherry tomatoes)
10 minutes
(mini focaccias)

450 g (1 lb) basic or
wholemeal pizza dough
(see recipes on pages 4-6)
flour for the work surface
2 spring onions
12 cherry tomatoes
1 clove of garlic
6 small cow's milk mozzarellas
1 handful of wild rocket
extra virgin olive oil
salt
freshly ground pepper

Preheat the oven to 100 °C (210 °F).

Halve the cherry tomatoes, arrange them cut side up on a baking sheet lined with parchment. Sprinkle with sliced garlic, salt and drizzle with extra virgin olive oil. Cook the tomatoes in the preheated oven for about 1 hour. Pat them with paper towels to remove any excess moisture and allow them to cool.

Raise the oven temperature to 220 °C (430 °F). Slice one of the spring onions and sauté it in a frying pan with a tablespoon of extra virgin olive oil and a pinch of salt.
Flatten the dough slightly on a floured work surface. Spread the cooked onion over it then roll it and knead it briefly to distribute the onion evenly throughout the dough. Divide the dough into 8-12 small balls. Dust them with flour and let them rise for 15 minutes.

Roll out each ball of dough to form a mini focaccia and place on the preheated pizza stone. Make an emulsion by combining 1 tablespoon of water and 1 tablespoon of extra virgin olive oil with a pinch of salt. Brush the dough with this mixture and promptly cook the focaccias for 10 minutes.

Top the focaccias with mozzarella halves, the cherry tomato confit, a few a few wild rocket leaves and a few ribbons cut from the remaining spring onion. Serve hot or warm.

Pizza with smoked scamorza cheese and poached egg

Preheat the oven to 250 °C (480 °F) with two individual pizza stones.

For **2** servings
Preparation:
10 minutes
Resting time:
15 minutes
Cooking time:
20 minutes

250 g (9 oz) basic pizza dough
(see recipes on pages 4-6)
10 thin slices of smoked
Scamorza cheese (or any
similar smoked cheese with
a texture like mozzarella)
2 tbsp tomato purée
1 purple spring onion
10 cherry tomatoes
12 small black olives
2 very fresh eggs
1 tbsp white vinegar
a few basil leaves
1 bunch of fresh
flat-leaf parsley
extra virgin olive oil
salt

Divide the dough into equal two equal portions forming two small balls. Let them rest for 15 minutes then flatten and stretch out the dough with your hands or a rolling pin on a floured work surface creating two discs.

Blanch the parsley in boiling water for 2 minutes. Drain the parsley and immerse it in ice water, then drain it again and chop it coarsely. Place the chopped parsley in a glass, add 2 tablespoons of water, 3 tablespoons of extra virgin olive oil and a pinch of salt. Emulsify with an immersion blender.

Transfer the discs of pizza dough to the two preheated pizza stones. Brush them with the tomato purée and cover them with the slices of cheese folding them in order to distribute them in a fan-like pattern. Add the finely sliced spring onion and bake in the preheated oven for 10 minutes.

In the meantime, bring a saucepan of water to a boil with the vinegar. Poach the eggs one at a time (about 3 minutes each). Drain them and immerse them in cold water for a few seconds to stop the cooking.

Dice the cherry tomatoes and season them with salt and a drizzle of extra virgin olive oil.

Spread the fresh tomato over the pizzas and return them to the oven for 2 minutes. Place an egg and basil leaves on each and put them back in the oven for 1 more minute.

Serve the pizzas sprinkled with the parsley emulsion.

Focaccia with mixed salad greens

For **4-6** servings
Preparation:
20 minutes
Cooking time:
10-12 minutes

250 g (9 oz) basic pizza dough
(see recipes on pages 4-6)
350 g (12 oz) ricotta
3 tbsp fresh cream
60 g (2 oz) roasted hazelnuts
150 g (5 ½ oz) mesclun
or mixed baby salad greens
cold pressed hazelnut oil
extra virgin olive oil
coarse sea salt
freshly ground pepper

Preheat the oven to 250 °C (480 °F).

Roll out the dough forming a disc with a diameter of 30 cm (12 in).
Prick the surface with a fork and transfer the dough to the preheated pizza stone.

Emulsify 3 tbsp of extra virgin olive oil, 3 tbsp of water and a pinch of salt. Quickly brush the dough with this mixture and bake the focaccia for 10-12 minutes in the preheated oven.

Wash and dry the salad leaves. Drizzle them with hazelnut oil and season with salt and pepper.

Mix the ricotta with the cream and the coarsely chopped hazelnuts.

Cut the focaccia into portions. Place a spoonful of ricotta and a bunch of seasoned salad leaves on each piece. Season generously with pepper and serve.

Pizza pockets

For **4** servings
Preparation:
20 minutes
Cooking time:
30 minutes
(vegetables)
10 minutes
(pizza)

400 g (14 oz) basic pizza
dough (see recipes
on pages 4-6)
200 g (7 oz) tomato purée
1 yellow onion
2 cloves of garlic
250 g (9 oz) green or white
cauliflower
2 tbsp pitted black olives
100 g (3 ½ oz) semi-mature
Pecorino (or Parmigiano)
basil
extra virgin olive oil
salt
hot red chili flakes
freshly ground pepper

Preheat the oven to 250 °C (480 °F).

Heat 2 tablespoons of oil in a frying pan with one clove of crushed unpeeled garlic. Add the tomato purée and 4 basil leaves and cook for 5 minutes on high heat to flavour the sauce. Remove it from the heat, add the salt and the hot red chili to taste. Allow to cool then eliminate the garlic.

Break off and discard the leaves from the cauliflower and divide the florets. Sauté them in a frying pan with the remaining clove of unpeeled garlic and 1 tablespoon of extra virgin olive oil.
Finely slice the onion and sauté it in a pan with 1 tablespoon of extra virgin olive oil and ½ a glass of water. Add salt once the water has evaporated and allow the onions to just begin to colour.

Divide the dough into 4 equal portions. Roll out each forming a thin rectangle. Distribute (in order) the tomato sauce, the onion, the olives, the cauliflower and the thinly sliced Pecorino cheese on each rectangle mounding the ingredients toward the middle. Fold the dough over the filling as though you were folding a letter. Crimp the edges to seal the pocket.

Transfer the 4 pockets to the preheated pizza stone. Brush them with an emulsion of extra virgin olive oil and water and bake them in the preheated oven for 10 minutes. If the dough is still pale and soft, bake them for a few more minutes.

Serve the pockets immediately, seasoned to taste with freshly ground black pepper or hot red chili.

Double mozzarella pizza

For 2-4 servings
Preparation:
10 minutes
Resting time:
15 minutes
Cooking time:
15 minutes

250 g (9 oz) basic pizza dough
(see recipes on pages 4-6)
8 thin slices of mozzarella
(or provola*)
100 g (3 ½ oz) tomato purée
6 small tomatoes
1 spring onion
200 g (7 oz) buffalo milk
mozzarella
2 sweet green peppers
2 tbsp black olives
2 sprigs of basil
1 sprig of dried oregano
extra virgin olive oil
salt
freshly ground pepper

*See note on page 18

Preheat the oven to 250 °C (480 °F) with two individual pizza stones.

Divide the dough into two equal parts. Cover them and let them rise for 15 minutes. Roll them out on a floured work surface forming two discs roughly the same size as the pizza stones.

Transfer the discs of dough to the preheated pizza stones and brush them with the tomato purée seasoned with salt and a drizzle of extra virgin olive oil. Bake in the preheated oven for 5 minutes.

Remove the pizzas from the oven and top them with the slices of mozzarella or provola cheese, the tomatoes in quarters, the black olives and the sliced spring onion. Return to the oven for approximately 10 more minutes.

Just before serving, add the buffalo mozzarella cut into chunks, the peppers sliced and seasoned with a little oil and salt, a generous amount of basil, crumbled oregano and pepper to taste.

Vegetarian pizza
with mixed vegetable topping

For **2-4** servings
Preparation:
20 minutes
Cooking time:
20 minutes
(vegetables)
20 minutes
(pizza)

400 g (14 oz) basic or
wholemeal pizza dough
(see recipes on pages 4-6)
150 g (5 ½ oz) tomato purée
1 white onion
2 baby carrots
1 aubergine/eggplant
½ red pepper/capiscum
½ yellow pepper/capiscum
2 courgettes/zucchini
8 small mozzarellas
1 bunch of fresh basil
1 tbsp sherry vinegar
extra virgin olive oil
salt
freshly ground pepper

Preheat the oven to 200 °C (400 °F).

Peel the vegetables and cut them into large pieces. Season them with 2-3 tablespoons of extra virgin olive oil and spread them on a baking tray lined with parchment. Cook the vegetables in the oven until they are tender (approximately 20 minutes). While they are still hot, season them with salt, pepper and the sherry vinegar.

Raise the oven temperature to 220 °C (430 °F).
With your hands or a rolling pin flatten and stretch out the dough on a floured work surface forming a disc roughly the same size as the pizza stone. Spread with a thin layer of the tomato purée.

Transfer the dough to the preheated pizza stone and bake for 20 minutes or until it is well cooked and golden. Top with the mixed vegetables and return it to the oven for a few minutes to heat through.

Once removed from the oven you may top the pizza with fresh mozzarella (divided in half) drizzled with extra virgin olive oil and seasoned with pepper and basil leaves.

If you omit the cheese, this pizza is perfect for vegans.

Mini focaccias with scallops

For **4** servings
Preparation:
10 minutes
Resting time:
15 minutes
Cooking time:
18 minutes

250 g (9 oz) basic pizza dough
(see recipes on pages 4-6)
8 scallops
8 thin slices of smoked
pancetta (or smoked bacon)
16 cherry tomatoes
1 bunch of mixed herbs
(parsley, basil, mint, fennel
fronds or dill and chives)
extra virgin olive oil
salt
freshly ground pepper

Preheat the oven to 200°C (390°F).

Divide the dough into 8 small balls and let them rest for 15 minutes. Roll them out creating 8 thin oval-shaped focaccias. Transfer these to a lightly oiled pizza stone. Brush them with an emulsion made from equal parts of extra virgin olive oil and water seasoned with a little salt.

Top the focaccias with the cherry tomatoes cut in half and salted separately. Bake immediately for 10-12 minutes or until the focaccias become golden and crisp.

Pat the scallops dry and wrap each in a slice of pancetta. Dry fry them for 30 seconds on each side, then set them aside on paper towels.
Place a scallop on each mini focaccia and return them to the oven for 3 minutes. In the meantime, place the herbs in a glass and mince them with scissors. Drizzle with olive oil and mix well.

Place a small serving of herbs beside each scallop. Season with pepper and serve immediately.

Pizza with Belgian endive, Gorgonzola, walnuts and dill

For **6** servings
Preparation:
10 minutes
Resting time:
15 minutes
+ 10 minutes
after baking
Cooking time:
40 minutes

450 g (1 lb) basic or
wholemeal pizza dough
(see recipes on pages 4-6)
200 g (7 oz) mature
Gorgonzola
(or Roquefort or similar
 variety of blue cheese)
4 tbsp grated Parmigiano
150 ml ($^2/_3$ cup) fresh cream
15 shelled walnuts
2 heads of Belgian endive/
chicory
3 sprigs of dill
1 small tray of sprouts of your
choice (watercress, rocket,
sunflower, etc.)
extra virgin olive oil
salt
freshly ground pepper

Preheat the oven to 220 °C (430 °F).

Use your hands or a rolling pin to flatten and stretch the dough on a floured sheet of baking parchment to form a disc a little smaller than the pizza stone. Let the dough rest for 15 minutes.

Cut the Gorgonzola into cubes. Mix the fresh cream with the grated Parmigiano. Finely chop half of the walnuts and add them to the cream mixture (if the texture becomes too thick, thin it with 1 or 2 tablespoons of cream).

Transfer the dough to the preheated pizza stone. Insert the Gorgonzola cheese cubes quickly into the dough, pressing them in with your finger to cover them completely in dough. Bake in the hot oven for 20 minutes.

Remove the pizza and spread the entire surface with the cream, walnut and cheese mixture. Complete cooking for another 15-20 minutes in the oven, taking care that the pizza does not become too dark (in the event, cover it with a sheet of baking parchment).

In the meantime, wash the heads of Belgian endive/chicory, discarding any wilted leaves. Slice them into rings and mix them with the remaining walnuts (roughly chopped), dill, sprouts and a drizzle of extra virgin olive oil. Season with salt just before use.

When the pizza is cooked, let it rest for 10 minutes before topping it with the salad. Sprinkle with pepper to taste and serve.

This pizza is also excellent served cold.

Traditional pizza with pancetta

For **4** servings
Preparation:
10 minutes
Resting time:
about 1 hour
and 30 minutes
Cooking time:
5 minutes (pancetta)
45 minutes (pizza)

450 g (1 lb) basic pizza dough
(see recipes on pages 4-6)
3 egg yolks
2 tbsp sugar
3 oz grated Pecorino
(or Parmigiano)
150 g (5 ¹/₂ oz) pancetta
or guanciale (or streaky bacon
or cheek bacon)
1 organic lemon
extra virgin olive oil
salt
freshly ground pepper

Preheat the oven to 220 °C (430 °F).

Dice the pancetta and brown it in a dry frying pan. Drain it and pat it dry with paper towels.

Stretch out the dough gently on a floured work surface. Grate the lemon distributing the rind over the dough with the sugar and the grated Pecorino. Lightly beat two egg yolks with a fork and spread them over the dough.

Roll up the dough and knead it well to mix the ingredients evenly throughout. It will gradually turn a pale yellow colour. Flatten it out again and spread the still warm pancetta over it. Roll it up and knead it only as much as necessary for the pancetta to be distributed evenly.

Form a ball with the dough and press it to give it a roughly long and flat shape. Cover it and let it rise until it doubles in volume.

Transfer the pizza to the preheated pizza stone. Brush it with the single remaining egg yolk and transfer to the hot oven. After 5 minutes, lower the temperature to 200 °C (390 °F) and continue baking for 40 minutes. The bottom of the pizza should appear hard and golden, and it will sound hollow like a loaf of bread when you tap it.

In order to prevent the surface from burning, once half of the cooking time has elapsed, check to see how the pizza is colouring and, if necessary, cover it with a sheet of damp baking parchment.

This traditional pizza should be served sliced, accompanied with pickles, vegetables preserved in oil and sliced cold meats of your choice.

Potato and salt cod pizza

For **4** servings
Preparation:
10 minutes
Cooking time:
17 minutes
(salt cod, potato)
33 minuti
(pizza)

350 g (12 oz) basic pizza
dough (see recipes
on pages 4-6)
2 cloves of garlic
2 boiled potatoes
250 g (9 oz) of desalted
salt cod (baccalà)
10 cherry tomatoes
1 teaspoon of chopped parsley
a few sprigs of thyme
extra virgin olive oil
salt

Preheat the oven to 220°C (430°F).

Cut the boned and skinned salt cod into pieces. Place it in a small frying pan with 3 tablespoons of water, a garlic clove and 3 tablespoons of oil. Cook the fish on medium heat for 10 minutes, repeatedly spooning the cooking liquid over it. Add more water if it dries out. Season it with the chopped parsley and thyme and break it up with a fork before setting it aside.

Roll out the dough forming an oval.

Slice the potatoes and sauté them in a frying pan with a clove of garlic and 3 tablespoons of extra virgin olive oil. Salt them lightly.
Arrange the potato slices on the pizza. Cut the cherry tomatoes in half and cook them in the same pan with a little salt and 2 tablespoons of water. When they start to shrivel, place them on the pizza, alternating them with the potato slices. Brush the edge of the dough with the cooking liquid.

Transfer the pizza to the preheated pizza stone. Bake for 30 minutes in the hot oven. Top it with the salt cod, return it to the oven for 3 more minutes and serve promptly.

Pizza with smoked herring salad topping

For **4** servings
Preparation:
15 minutes
Restsing time:
15 minutes
Cooking time:
20 minutes

350 g (12 ¹/₂ oz) basic slow-rising or wholemeal pizza dough (see recipes on page 6)
150 g (5 ¹/₂ oz) tomato purée
120 g (4 ¹/₂ oz) peeled and cooked beetroot
4 small slices of raw beetroot
4 hard-boiled eggs
150 g (5 ¹/₂ oz) vacuum-packed smoked herring
6 fresh radishes with their leaves
100 g (3 ¹/₂ oz) full-fat natural yoghurt
100 g (3 ¹/₂ oz) sour cream
extra virgin olive oil
salt
freshly ground pepper

Preheat the oven to 220 °C (430 °F).

Dice the cooked beetroot and blend it with the tomato purée, 2 large pinches of salt and 1 tablespoon of extra virgin olive oil.

With your hands or a rolling pin flatten the dough forming a disc that is a little smaller than the pizza stone. Transfer the dough to the preheated pizza stone and dust it with flour. Spread it with the beetroot sauce. Brush the edges with extra virgin olive oil and bake in the hot oven for 20 minutes.

In the meantime, peel and slice the hard-boiled eggs, cut the herring into small pieces and cut the raw beetroot into julienne strips.

Wash and drain the green and tender radish leaves and slice the radishes finely with a mandoline. Season the radishes, radish leaves and the julienned raw beetroot with a drizzle of extra virgin olive oil and salt.

When the pizza is cooked and golden, remove from the oven. Wait 5 minutes before topping it with the freshly seasoned salad, the sliced egg and the herring pieces. Finish with a sprinkling of freshly ground pepper and a drizzle of extra virgin olive oil.

Blend the sour cream and yoghurt and serve as an accompaniment.

Sweet pizza

Preheat the oven to 220 °C (430 °F).

For **6-8** servings
Preparation:
5 minutes
Resting time:
15 minutes
Cooking time:
30-40 minutes

400 g (14 oz) wholemeal
pizza dough
(see recipe on page 6)
50 g (1 ³/₄ oz) unsalted butter
4 tbsp dark brown sugar

Serve with:
2 small punnets of
strawberries (450 g/1 lb)
450 g (1 lb) vanilla ice cream

Roll out the dough on a floured work surface and let it rest for 15 minutes. Transfer the dough to the preheated and floured pizza stone. Using your fingertips, press the dough to make a circular channel 1 centimetre (¹/₂ inch) from the edge (to prevent the butter from running off while baking).

Dot the entire surface of the pizza with small pieces of butter and sprinkle it with the sugar.

Bake in the hot oven for 30-40 minutes. Check how the dough is cooking by lifting it slightly from the pizza stone with a spatula. If the bottom is not golden and dry, continue to bake the pizza for a few more minutes.

Allow the sweet pizza to cool for 15 minutes before cutting it. Serve it with ice cream and strawberries.

This pizza is also excellent cold and may be accompanied with an apple and cinnamon or pear and cardamom compote or with blueberry jam.

This recipe may be made lactose-free by replacing the butter with extra virgin olive oil, reducing the quantity by one third and by substituting the traditional ice cream with a soy-based product.

Grape focaccia

For **8** servings
Preparation:
10 minutes
Resting time:
15 minutes
Cooking time:
30 minutes

450 g (1 lb) slow rising pizza
dough (see recipe on page 6)
500 g (1 ⅛ lb) purple
or red grapes (preferably
a wine grape variety)
80 g (3 oz) granulated
or Demerara sugar
extra virgin olive oil

Preheat the oven to 220 °C (430 °F).

Roll out the dough to form a rectangle. Separate the grapes and wash and dry them. Distribute half of the grapes over one half of the dough. Sprinkle generously with sugar and fold the other half of the dough over the grapes enclosing them. Allow to rest for 15 minutes.

Transfer the focaccia to the lightly oiled pizza stone. Press it with your palms to flatten and spread the dough out again, this time in a roughly circular shape. Arrange the remaining grapes on the surface, pressing them into the dough with your fingers. Sprinkle with sugar and drizzle generously with extra virgin olive oil.

Bake in the hot oven for 30 minutes. Check how the dough is cooking by lifting the base slightly with a spatula. If it is dry and a light golden colour, remove the focaccia from the oven. If not, continue to bake for about 10 more minutes. Serve cold.

If this focaccia is made with slow-rising dough, it will keep well for 2-3 days wrapped in waxed paper and in a thick tea towel.

Index